A GIFT FOR

Tom

÷ FROM ÷

Vivian

— 2000

Love
Isn't Easy

by

SCHULZ

BOOKS

HarperCollins*Publishers*

BOK 4009

Love
Lessons

SURE, CHUCK...IN THE MEANTIME, HERE'S ANOTHER ONE...SAY A PERSON HAS KIND OF A BIG NOSE, AND ANOTHER PERSON CALLS HER "BASEBALL NOSE," AND TELLS HER NOT TO GO NEAR THE BALL PARK 'CAUSE SOMEONE MIGHT AUTOGRAPH HER NOSE, SHOULD SHE BE OFFENDED?

WHAT DO YOU THINK, CHUCK?

G SHOULDN'T GET INVOLVED, AND AN AUTOGRAPH ON A NOSE WOULD PROBABLY WASH OFF...

ALTHOUGH, IN THE LONG RUN, IT ALSO COULD SAVE YOU A LOT OF TROUBLE...

The
Art Of Love
Letters

The Art Of Love Letters

 # The Art Of Love Letters

NOTHING IMPORTANT

 **The Art Of Love Letters**

 # The Art Of Love Letters

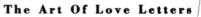

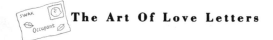

If you aren't as cute as you used to be, send it back.

You Say Nēither, I Say Nēither...

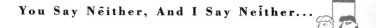

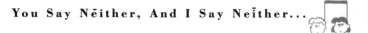

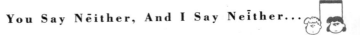

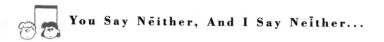

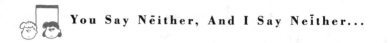

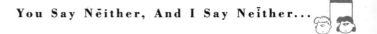

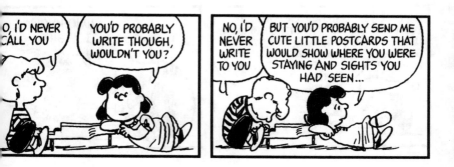

I HAVE BEAUTIFUL
MEMORIES OF OTHER SUMMER
NIGHTS JUST LIKE THIS...

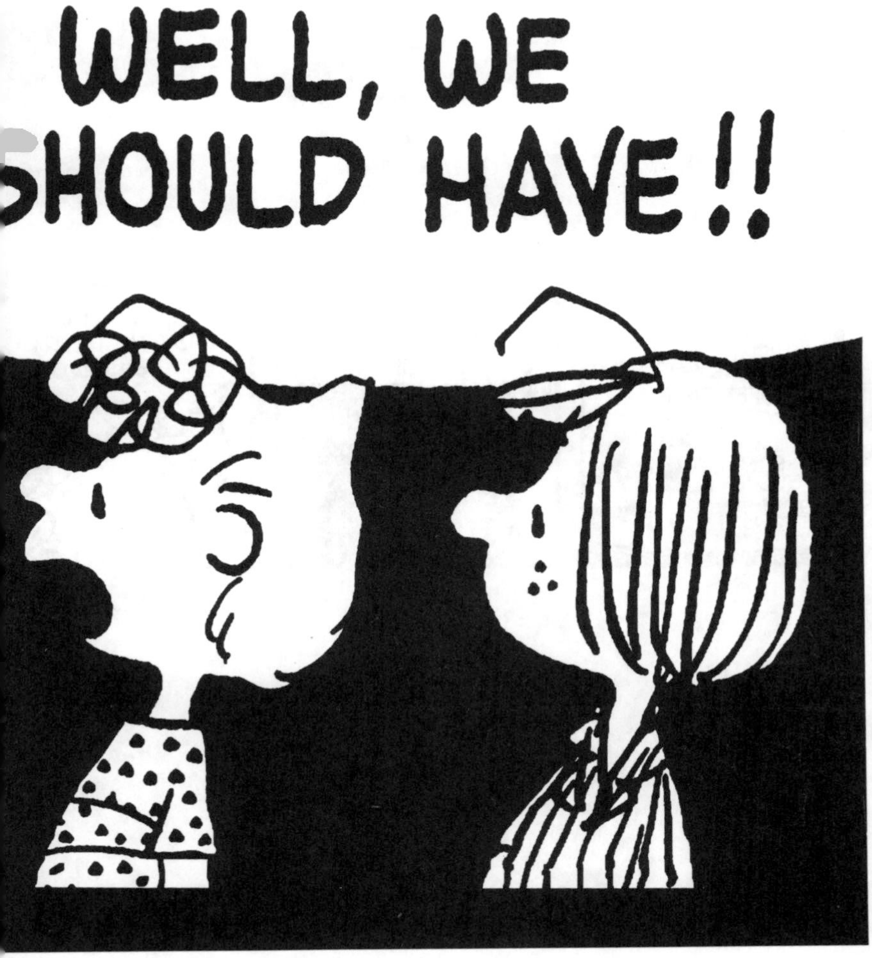
WELL, WE SHOULD HAVE!!

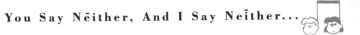

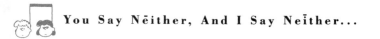

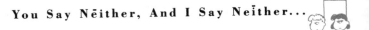

Who's Jealous?

Who's Jealous?

WHO ARE YOU, AND WHY ARE YOU WALKING WITH MY SWEET BABBOO?

I'M NOT HER SWEET BABBOO!

MY NAME IS TAPIOCA PUDDING.

MY DAD IS IN LICENSING..
MY FACE IS GOING TO
BE ON T-SHIRTS AND
LUNCH BOXES..

IT'D LOOK A
LOT BETTER ON
A DOG DISH!

Love's
Labors
Lost

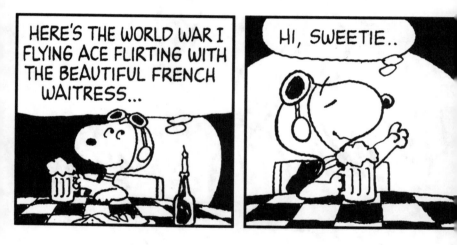

 **Love's Labors Lost**

Love's Labors Lost

I, THERE..MY NAME IS LINUS.. I LIEVE WE HAVE A FRIEND IN COMMON..

HIS NAME IS CHARLIE BROWN..HE SITS ACROSS THE ROOM FROM YOU IN SCHOOL.. NO, BY THE WINDOWS..NEAR THE PENCIL SHARPENER..NO, IN THE LAST ROW...

 **Love's Labors Lost**

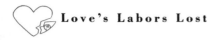

First published 1996 by Collins Publishers
Published under license from HarperCollins Publishers Inc.
Conceived and produced by Packaged Goods Incorporated
276 Fifth Avenue, New York, NY 10001
A Quarto Company

Based on the PEANUTS ® comic strip by Charles M. Schulz
http://www.snoopy.com
Library of Congress Cataloging-in-Publication Data
Schulz, Charles M.
(Peanuts. Selections)
Love isn't easy / by Schulz.
p. cm.
"A Packaged Goods Incorporated Book"—T.P. verso
ISBN 0-00-225148-5
1. Title
PN6728.P4S32465   1996
741.5'973—dc20   96-19377
                                                   CIP0